PERSONAL BONDS!

The Chemistry of **Our Bodies**

Written by Joseph P. Cataliotti

WORLD BOOK

www.worldbook.com

Co-published by agreement between Shi Tu Hui and World Book, Inc.

Shi Tu Hui
Room 1807, Block 1,
#3 West Dawang Road
Chaoyang District, Beijing 100025
P.R. China

World Book, Inc.
180 North LaSalle Street
Suite 900
Chicago, Illinois 60601
USA

© 2026. All rights reserved. This volume may not be reproduced in whole or in part in any form without prior written permission from the publisher.

WORLD BOOK and the GLOBE DEVICE are registered trademarks or trademarks of World Book, Inc.

Library of Congress Control Number: 2025942242

Aha! Academy: Chemistry
ISBN: 978-0-7166-7346-0 (set, hardcover)

Personal Bonds! The Chemistry of Our Bodies
ISBN: 978-0-7166-7355-2 (hard cover)
ISBN: 978-0-7166-7375-0 (e-book)
ISBN: 978-0-7166-7365-1 (soft cover)

Staff

Editorial

Vice President
Tom Evans

Senior Manager, New Content
Jeff De La Rosa

Associate Manager, New Content
William D. Adams

Senior Curriculum Designer
Caroline Davidson

Curriculum Designer
Mikayla Kightlinger

Proofreader
Nathalie Strassheim

Indexer
Nathaniel Lindstrom

Graphics and Design

Senior Visual
Communications Designer
Melanie Bender

Designer
Shannon Hagman

Written by Joseph P. Cataliotti

Acknowledgments

The publishers gratefully acknowledge the following sources for photography. All illustrations were prepared by WORLD BOOK unless otherwise noted.

Cover: ART-ur/Shutterstock; cones/Shutterstock; ASDF_MEDIA/Shutterstock; Komsan Loonprom/Shutterstock; PeopleImages.com - Yuri A/Shutterstock

© Henry Westheim Photography/Alamy 42; © Nemes Laszlo/Alamy 39; © Science Photo Library/Alamy 13, 28, 32, 34, 38, 46; © World History Archive/Alamy 27; © PEDRE/Getty Images 33; Harold B. Lee Library 39; Jacek Proszyk (licensed under CC0 1.0) 23; Jynto (licensed under CC0 1.0) 46; Nephron (licensed under CC BY-SA 3.0) 21; © Steve Gschmeissner, SPL/Photo Researchers 37; Public Domain (NIAID) 46; © Public Domain 7, 11, 20, 41, 46; © INNERSPACE IMAGING/Science Source 33; © Shutterstock 3, 4, 5, 6, 7, 8, 9, 10, 11, 12, 13, 14, 15, 16, 17, 18, 19, 20, 21, 22, 23, 24, 25, 26, 27, 28, 29, 30, 31, 32, 33, 34, 35, 36, 37, 38, 39, 40, 41, 42, 43, 44, 45, 46, 47, 48; Wellcome Library (licensed under CC BY 4.0) 11

There is a glossary of terms on page 48. Terms defined in the glossary are in type that looks like *this* on their first appearance on any spread (two facing pages).

Contents

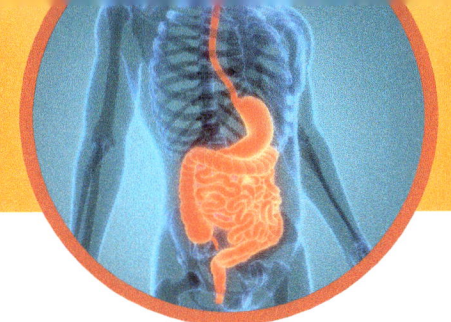

Introduction 4

1 Energy from food 6
Digesting dinner 8
Vital molecule: hydrochloric acid 10

2 Life from air 12
Respiration 14
Vital protein: hemoglobin 16

3 The human body 18
Liver 20
Kidneys 22
Vitamins 24

4 Building up & breaking down 26
DNA's code 28
RNA, the sidekick 30
Building bones 32
Apoptosis 34

5 Chemistry of medicine 36
Aspirin 38
Penicillin and antibiotics 40
Chemotherapy 42

An egg-shell-ent experiment 44
Index 46
Glossary 48

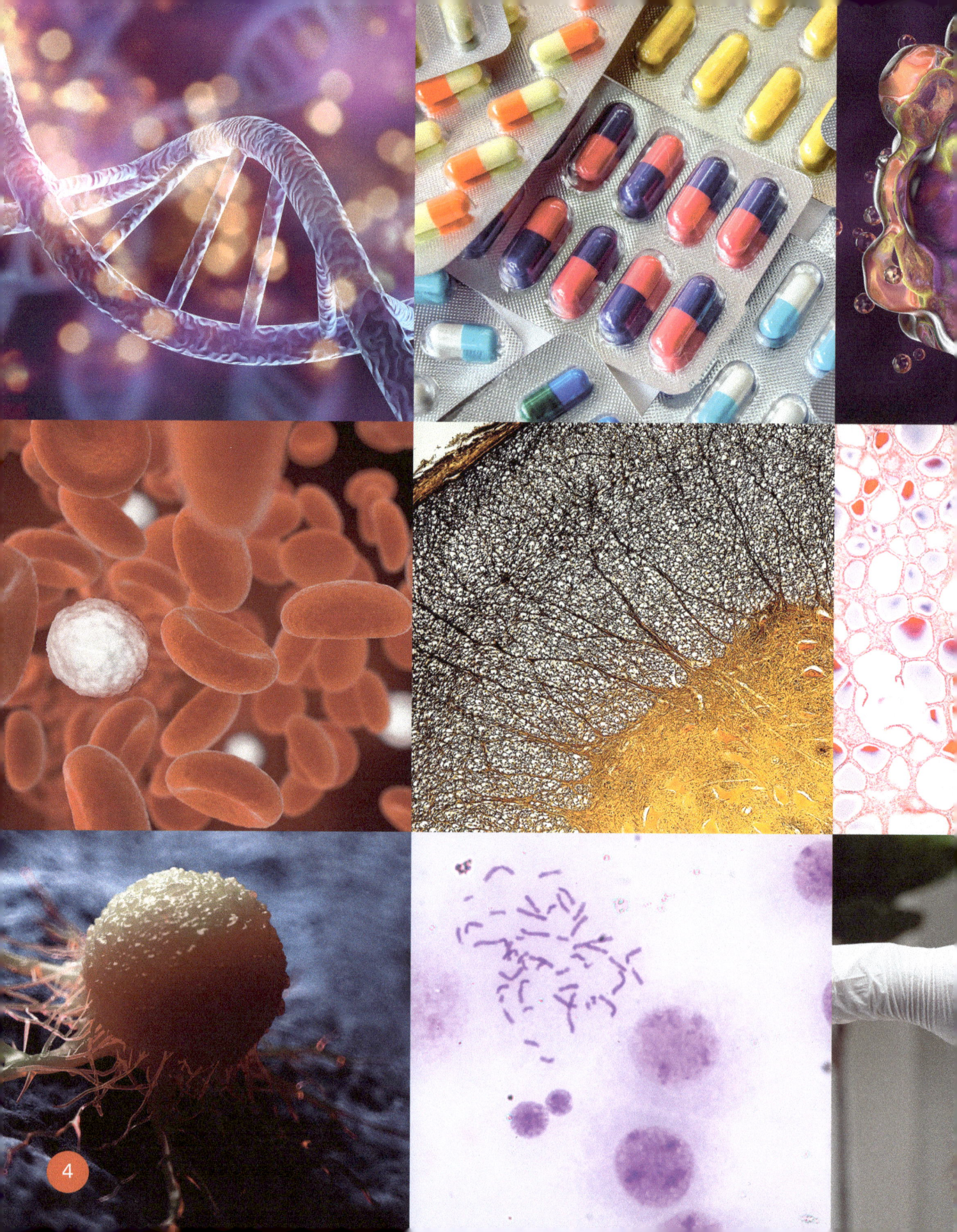

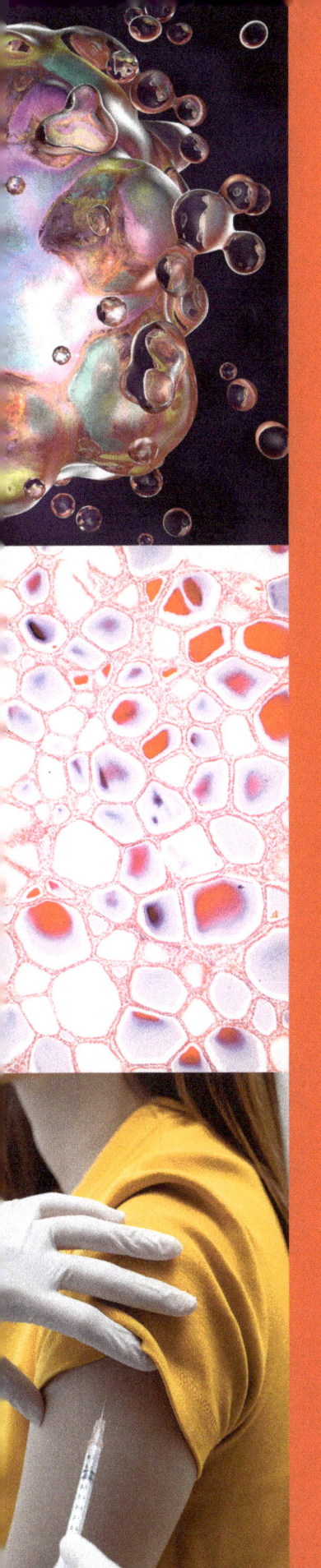

Introduction

Your body can be thought of as a chemical factory. Your digestive system breaks down food into materials to build new *cells* and fuel to power you throughout your day and keep your brain running. Complex *proteins* carry out an endless sequence of chemical tasks, working like microscopic machines. And *DNA*, a unique *molecule* found in nearly every cell of your body, guides all of these processes.

Your body—from the sub-microscopic molecules that make up your cells to the eyes you're using to read this book—can all be understood in terms of chemistry: the scientific study of the substances that make up our world and the rules that describe how they react with one another.

Eye see chemistry!

1
ENERGY FROM FOOD

From the moment you take a bite of your food, saliva in your mouth begins breaking it down. Swallowed food travels down the esophagus into the stomach. In the stomach, food is digested by hydrochloric *acid* (HCl), a highly corrosive chemical. After the stomach, food passes into the intestines, where other *chemicals* break it down further. After it passes through the large intestine, the body disposes of the remaining waste.

Food is the body's fuel. Your body chemically processes the food you eat by passing it through a veritable conveyor belt of *organs*.

Molecules can come together or break apart in processes called chemical *reactions*. Chemical reactions play a role in all the changes that take place within the human body.

During digestion, the body breaks down food into its various building blocks: *molecules* and *atoms*. All things, including you, are made of minuscule atoms, for example *oxygen* and *hydrogen*. These atoms come together to form molecules, including *water*. A molecule of water, also known as H_2O, has one oxygen atom and two hydrogen atoms.

DID YOU KNOW?

Your stomach only has one compartment, but a cow's stomach has four! All that extra hardware helps the cow to digest tough, chewy grass.

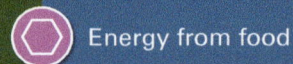 Energy from food

Digesting dinner

Digestion begins not in the stomach, but in the mouth! Chewing breaks your food into smaller parts that are easier to digest. Amylase, an *enzyme* in saliva, breaks down some starches to sugar. An enzyme is a *molecule* that speeds up *chemical reactions* in living things.

Next, the partly digested food passes into the small intestine. There, the digestive process is completed by pancreatic juice, intestinal juice, and bile. Pancreatic and intestinal juices contain enzymes that break down partly digested proteins, change starch into simple sugars, and split apart fats. Bile, which comes from the liver, contains chemicals that help further break down and absorb fats.

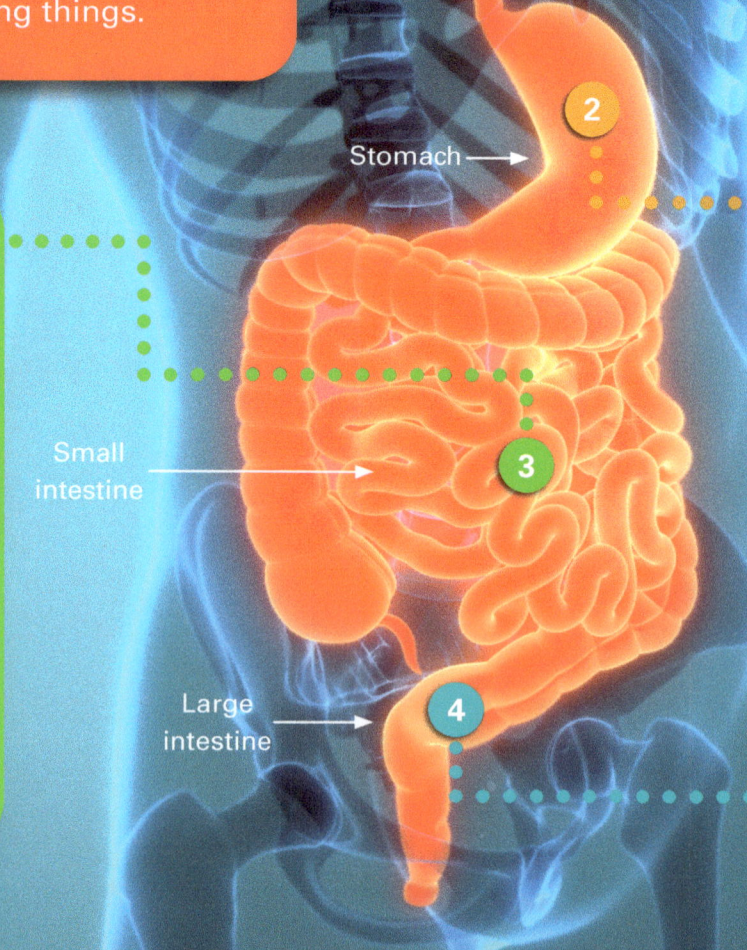

Trachea

Stomach

Small intestine

Large intestine

What happens after you eat a meal?

During digestion, the body pulls the important bits from your food and gets rid of the rest.

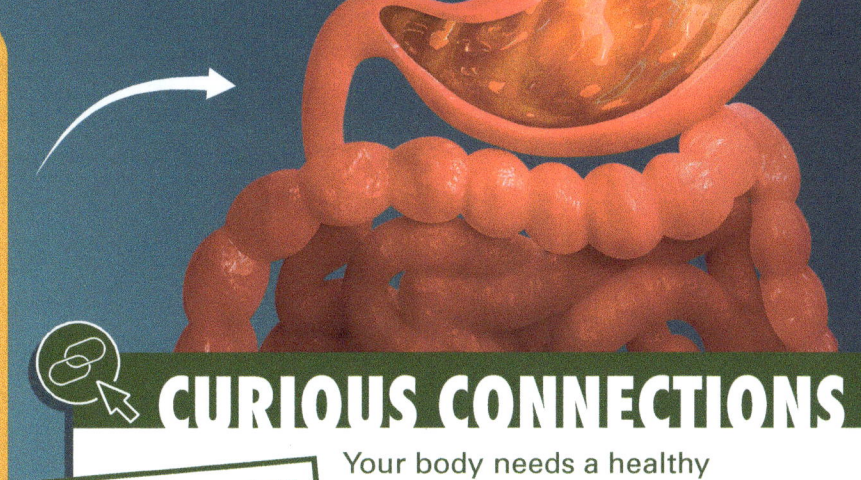

When you swallow your food, it plummets down the esophagus and into your stomach. There, the muscular organ churns food with a fluid called gastric juice. Gastric juice contains hydrochloric *acid* and the enzyme pepsin. This juice begins the digestion of *protein* from such foods as meat, eggs, milk, nuts, and some vegetables.

CURIOUS CONNECTIONS

NUTRITION Your body needs a healthy balance of fats, proteins, and carbohydrates to function. It may use carbohydrates for quick energy, fats as a more stable energy source, and proteins to build new cells and tissues.

Waste products, the leftovers of digestion, pass into your large intestine. Some additional processes happen there, with the action of bacteria making the final waste product: feces.

Energy from food

Vital molecule: hydrochloric acid

STATS

Symbol
HCl

Melting point
-174.6 °F (-115.8 °C)

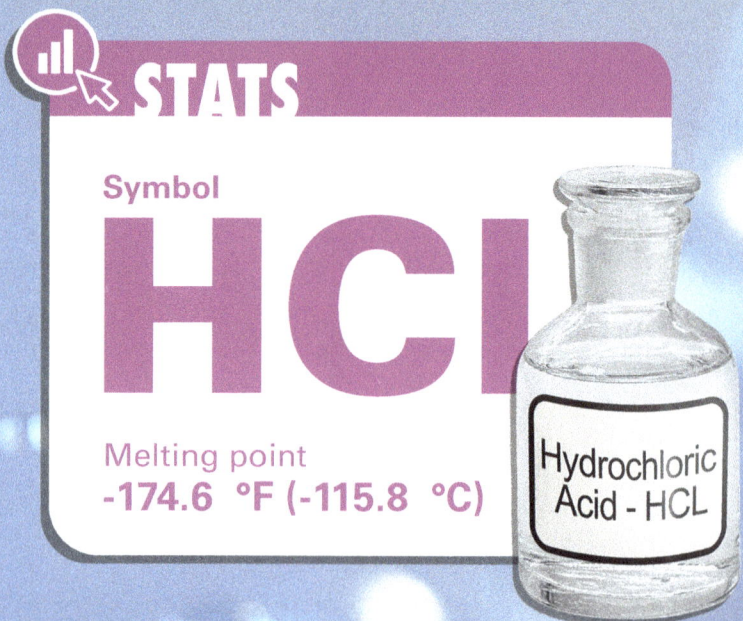

Hydrochloric acid is a dangerous chemical that has many important uses. The acid is a colorless liquid with an irritating odor. It fumes when exposed to air. Hydrochloric acid is highly corrosive and can cause serious burns.

HCl may be dangerous, but your body uses small amounts of it to digest food. Most of the time this is no problem—a mucous lining protects the walls of the stomach, and damaged cells there are easily replaced. But if the stomach's natural balance becomes upset, HCl can damage the stomach lining, producing sores called ulcers. The painful sensation known as heartburn happens when hydrochloric acid rises out of the stomach and into the esophagus.

Hydrochloric *acid* is a powerful and dangerous *chemical*. It's in your stomach right now—but don't worry, it's supposed to be there!

From the 800's to the 1400's, scholarship flourished in the Middle East, and Arabic-speaking scientists made many contributions to science and mathematics, including the developing field of chemistry. Around the year 900, the physician **Al-Rāzī** described an early method to make hydrochloric acid.

A neat trick, but not a great medicine!

HCl is a simple *molecule:* one *atom* of *hydrogen* and one atom of chlorine, bound together. But it doesn't really function as an acid until that bond is broken. Confused yet? HCl and other acids dissolve in *water*. In fact, HCl is such an effective acid because it so easily splits apart in water. Its hydrogen atom can form new bonds, disrupting other molecules.

Hydrochloric acid has uses outside of breaking down the cheeseburger you just ate. It is used in industry in preparing many chemical compounds. The acid is also used in metallurgy and food processing.

11

2 LIFE FROM AIR

Elemental *oxygen* makes up over 20 percent of Earth's atmosphere. This is good news for us humans, because we use oxygen in important ***chemical reactions*** inside the body.

You're breathing right now. But why do humans and other animals breathe air?

When you breathe in, air travels to your lungs. There, oxygen passes through a thin wall of cells into tiny blood vessels filled with circulating blood. ***Hemoglobin***, a complex ***protein*** in red blood ***cells***, absorbs the oxygen, and red blood cells carry it all around the body.

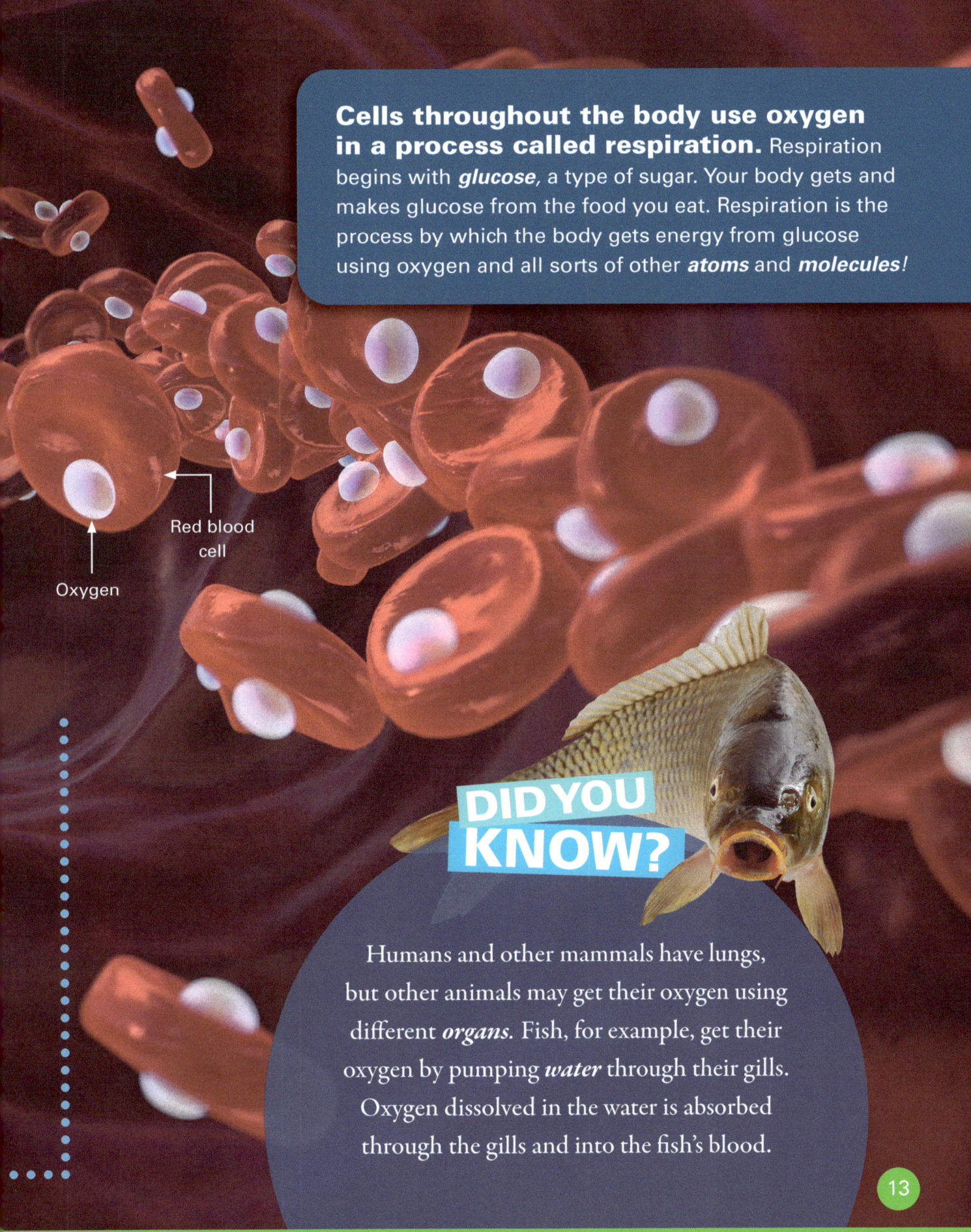

Cells throughout the body use oxygen in a process called respiration. Respiration begins with *glucose*, a type of sugar. Your body gets and makes glucose from the food you eat. Respiration is the process by which the body gets energy from glucose using oxygen and all sorts of other *atoms* and *molecules*!

Red blood cell

Oxygen

DID YOU KNOW?

Humans and other mammals have lungs, but other animals may get their oxygen using different *organs*. Fish, for example, get their oxygen by pumping *water* through their gills. Oxygen dissolved in the water is absorbed through the gills and into the fish's blood.

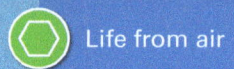
Life from air

Respiration

Respiration involves a series of chemical reactions by which the body's cells convert glucose—a sugar derived from food—and a bunch of other **molecules** into a molecule called adenosine triphosphate *(ATP)*. Your body uses ATP for energy.

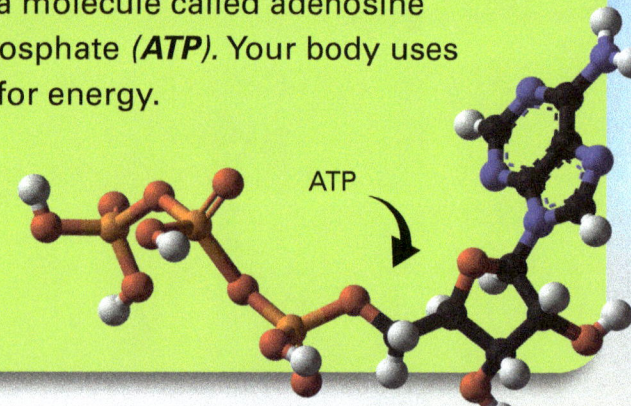
ATP

The first step in respiration is called glycolysis. Glycolysis means breaking down glucose. Starting with glucose and other molecules, your body produces ATP—but not much.

CURIOUS CONNECTIONS

EXERCISE SCIENCE When you run or perform another high-intensity workout, your cells don't have enough oxygen to make all the energy they need. Instead of the Krebs cycle, your body recycles the products of glycolysis to make more energy. This produces lactic *acid* in your muscles. This lactic acid quickly gets flushed from your muscles.

Using a series of complex *chemical reactions*, your body converts the air you breathe and the food you eat into energy.

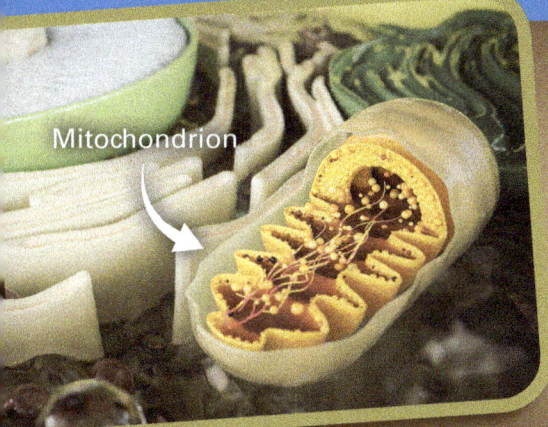

Mitochondrion

With oxygen, your body can produce much more energy. When oxygen is present, a cell can carry out a series of reactions that produce even more energy molecules from the products of glycolysis. This series of reactions is called the Krebs cycle. The Krebs cycle also makes carbon dioxide as a byproduct.

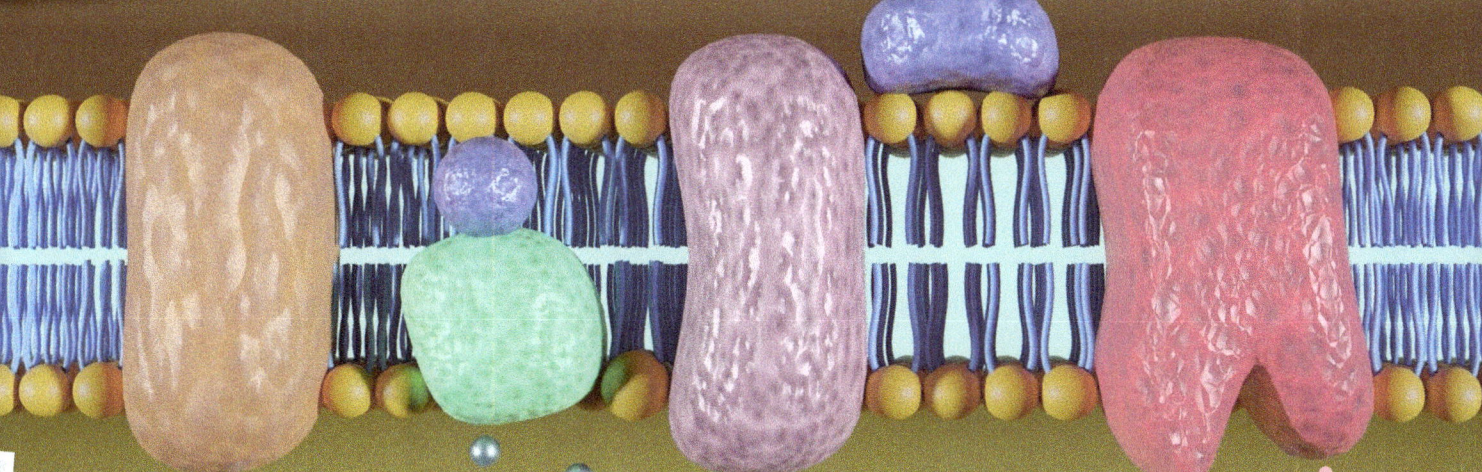

The next stage after the Krebs cycle is called the electron transport chain. This stage takes place in a part of the cell called the mitochondrion. Using electrons from ATP and other energy molecules, *proteins* pump positively charged *hydrogen atoms* into an area of the mitochondrion called the intermembrane space. This positively charged area passes hydrogen atoms back through a rotating protein, which uses the atoms to create ATP molecules—somewhat like flowing water turns the turbine of a dam. The electron transport chain results in 30 ATP molecules for each glucose used way back in glycolysis! At the end, oxygen atoms also take on the transported electrons and form *water*.

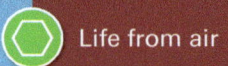
Life from air

Vital protein: hemoglobin

STATS

Abbreviation

Hb

Also known as
Hgb

Number of subunits
4

Number of O_2 molecules carried
4

Hemoglobin is a complex group of *protein molecules* found in red blood *cells.* Each one is made up of four globin proteins. Each globin corrals a molecule called heme that contains one iron atom. This atom serves as a binding point to *oxygen* molecules.

Red blood cells absorb oxygen as they move across the surface of tiny air sacs in the lungs called alveoli. Inside the red blood cells, the oxygen molecules bond to the iron molecules within the hemoglobin. As the red cells travel through the body, they release the oxygen into body tissues.

Imagine a food delivery truck that also picks up your trash! That's the kind of double duty that red blood cells pull! Hemoglobin bonds with carbon dioxide, too, so red blood cells pick up carbon dioxide as they travel around the body. The red blood cells return to the lungs and release the carbon dioxide molecules as they pick up more oxygen. You get rid of the carbon dioxide when you breathe out.

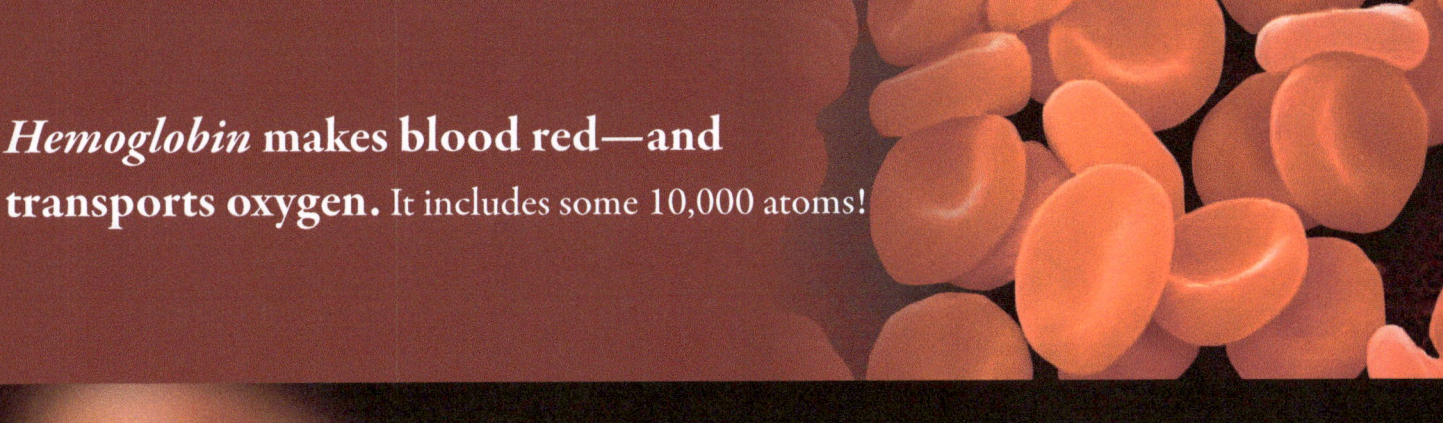

Hemoglobin makes blood red—and transports oxygen. It includes some 10,000 atoms!

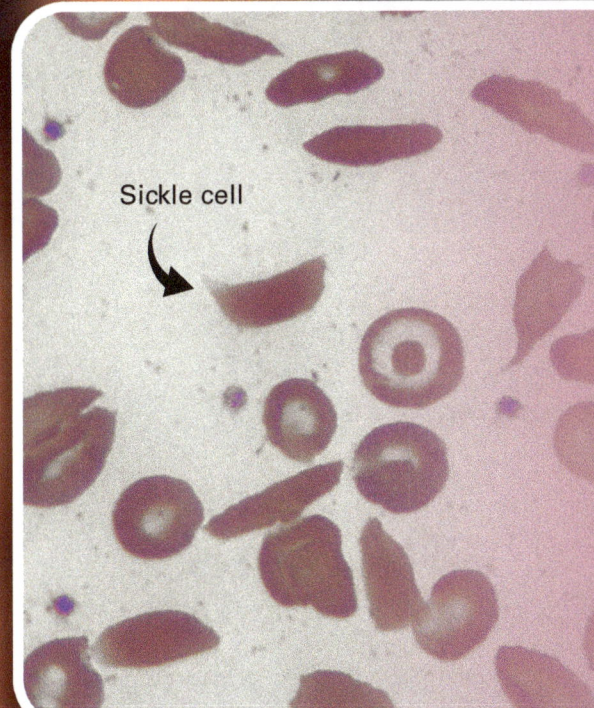

Sickle cell

With such a complex structure, there are plenty of things that can go wrong—or just differently—in the body's manufacture of hemoglobin! One variant, called hemoglobin S or sickle hemoglobin, makes those who have it resistant to the disease malaria. When two people with hemoglobin S have children, however, there's a chance the child will be born with a serious condition called sickle cell disease (SCD). The bodies of people with SCD make sticky, crescent-shaped red blood cells. These blood cells do not carry oxygen as well. Other SCD symptoms include periodic attacks of severe pain and fever and blood flow disruptions.

TECH TIME

Blood transfusions can save lives. But donated blood must be kept refrigerated and has a short shelf life. There's rarely enough to go around. As an alternative, researchers are developing artificial blood. One idea is to dispense with the red blood cells altogether and inject hemoglobin enzymes directly into the blood serum (liquid). These hemoglobin-based oxygen carriers (HBOC's) would remain efficient and stable over broader temperature ranges and longer timespans. But, the body's immune system attacks hemoglobin outside of red blood cells. Researchers are working to develop HBOC's that avoid these defense mechanisms.

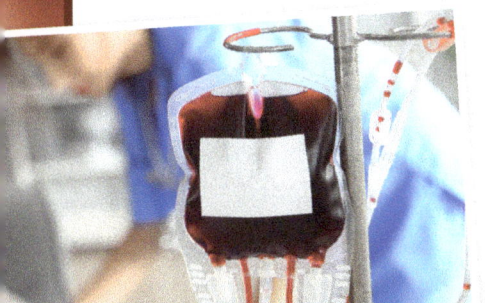

3
THE HUMAN BODY

The *cell* is the basic unit of living things. But you're not just a big lump of random cells! Cells of the same types tend to group together. Such a collection of cells is called a tissue. When two or more tissues come together, they form an ***organ***.

Liver tissue

It sounded like a good idea at the time!

The **ancient Greeks** thought the human body had four key fluids called humors. They believed an imbalance of these humors caused sicknesses. They were wrong! But, this idea was one of the launching points of medicine. Doctors and scientists spent centuries disproving this idea and coming up with better ones. That's how the scientific method works!

The human body is incredibly complex! It takes in resources—food, water, and oxygen—and produces all the chemicals it needs to survive and grow.

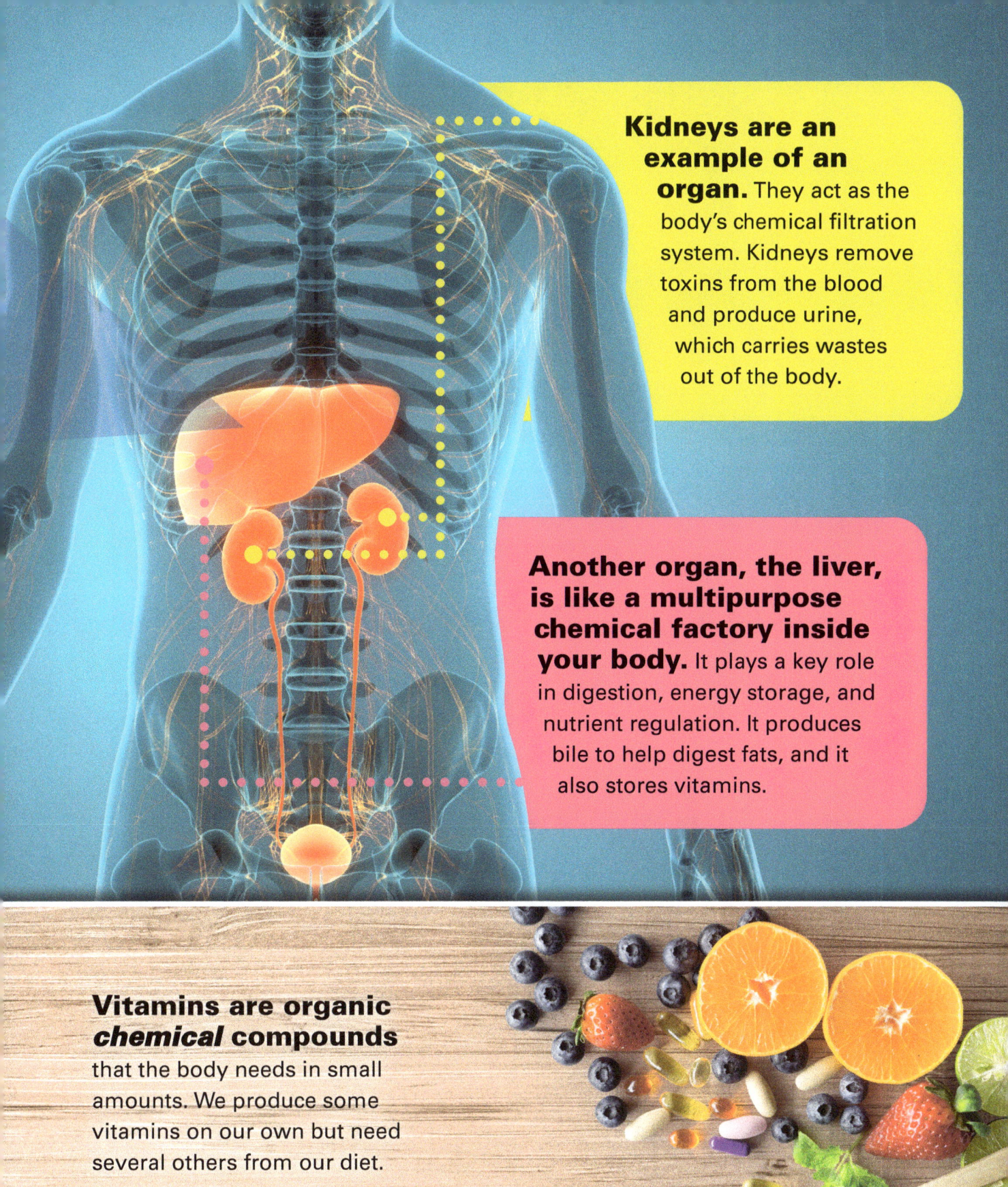

Kidneys are an example of an organ. They act as the body's chemical filtration system. Kidneys remove toxins from the blood and produce urine, which carries wastes out of the body.

Another organ, the liver, is like a multipurpose chemical factory inside your body. It plays a key role in digestion, energy storage, and nutrient regulation. It produces bile to help digest fats, and it also stores vitamins.

Vitamins are organic *chemical* compounds that the body needs in small amounts. We produce some vitamins on our own but need several others from our diet.

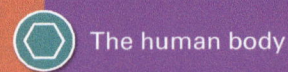
The human body

Liver

Your liver produces many key *molecules* your body needs to function. What keeps you from running out of energy long after you've digested food? The liver does!

Thanks to my liver, I can dance all day!

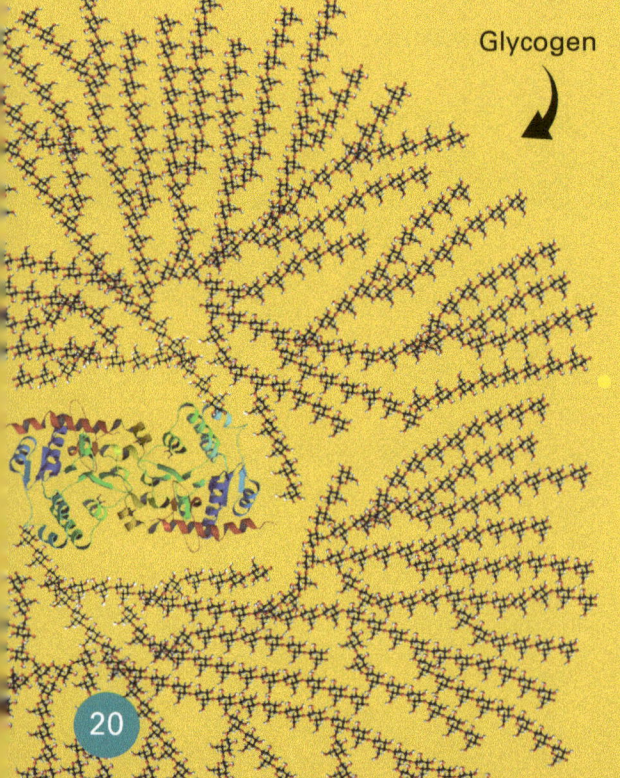

Glycogen

The liver acts as a major energy storehouse. It removes excess *glucose* from the blood and stores it in the form of a starchlike compound called glycogen. When the body needs energy, the liver converts glycogen back into glucose and releases it into the blood.

The liver also converts fatty *acids* (a kind of organic acid) and amino *acids* into glucose when its store of glycogen is low. In this way, the liver helps ensure that the cells of the body receive a constant supply of fuel—even when your last meal is a distant memory!

The liver is one of the most complex of all human *organs*. Your liver is a key part of your body's *chemical* factory.

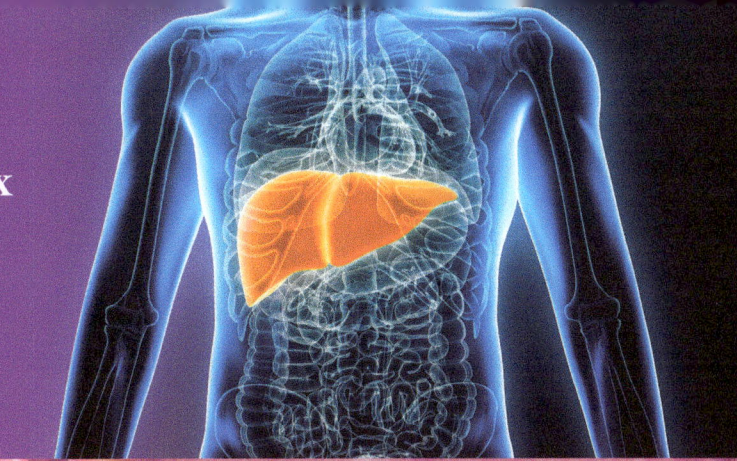

Bile

Conveniently located near your stomach, the liver also plays a key role in digestion. The liver secretes a greenish fluid called bile. This stinky liquid reduces the size of fat droplets, which helps *enzymes* in the intestine to split each fat molecule into a fatty acid and a molecule called glycerol.

The liver also plays an essential role in the storage of certain vitamins. The liver stores vitamin A, as well as vitamins D, E, and K and the vitamins of the B-complex group. It also stores iron and other minerals.

21

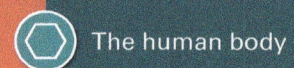 The human body

Kidneys

The kidneys are purplish-brown organs. They are shaped like beans and are about the size of an adult's fist.

Blood flows into each kidney. The kidney filters this blood, absorbing substances needed by the body. These include *amino acids*, *glucose*, and about 99 percent of the body's *water*. These substances then rejoin the blood.

The kidney takes substances that the body doesn't need—such as ammonia, urea, uric acid, and excess water—and sends them down to the bladder. That's what urine is! Urine carries various waste materials out of the body. If the kidneys fail to function, poisons can build up in the body, eventually causing death.

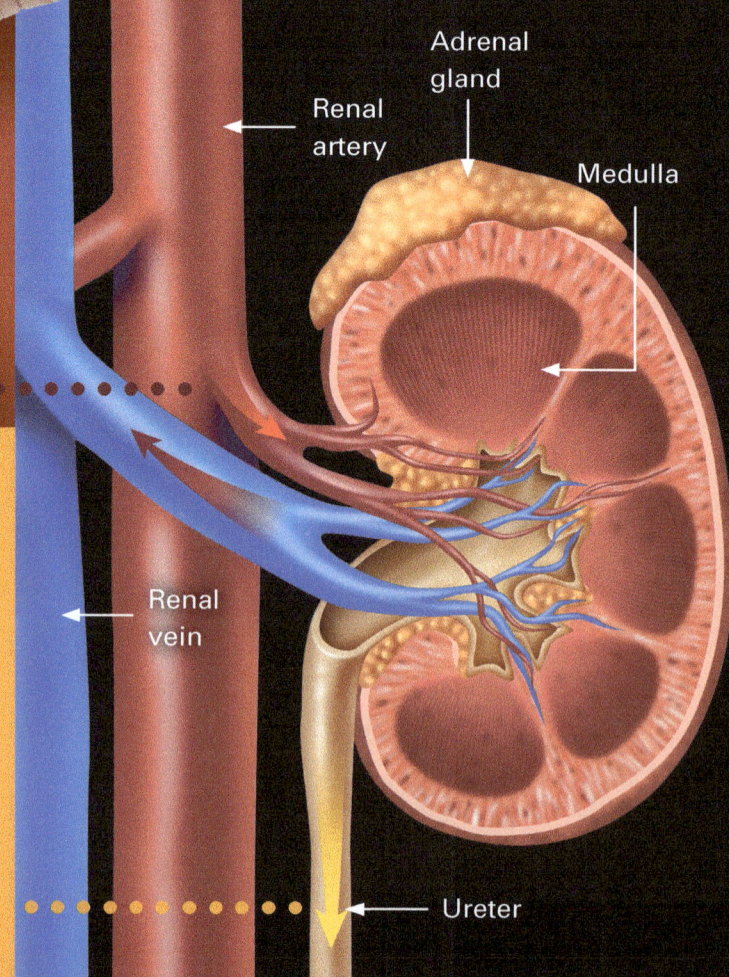

Your body also relies on your two kidneys for vital functions. Your kidneys serve as the blood's filtration system.

In addition to producing urine, the kidneys secrete a hormone called erythropoietin, which controls the production of red blood *cells*.

The kidneys convert vitamin D from an inactive to an active form. The active form is essential for normal bone development.

The kidneys also help maintain the body's blood pressure by releasing an enzyme called renin.

CURIOUS CONNECTIONS

MEDICINE Sometimes, waste can fuse with calcium to form objects in the kidney called kidney stones. Most kidney stones pass out of the kidney with urine—and plenty of pain. Other kidney stones require surgical intervention.

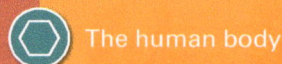
The human body

Vitamins

A vitamin is an organic *chemical* compound that the body needs in small amounts. Vitamins make up one of the major groups of nutrients, which are food substances necessary for growth and health.

Why are vitamins so important? Vitamins regulate the chemical *reactions* by which the body converts food into energy and living *tissue*.

Each vitamin has such specific uses— so one vitamin cannot replace another! Sometimes, however, the lack of one vitamin can interfere with the function of another. Over time, continued lack of one vitamin can result in a vitamin deficiency disease. Not good!

DID YOU KNOW?

Sailors throughout history have suffered from a disease called scurvy. As it turns out, scurvy can be avoided and even cured by eating regular servings of fruits and vegetables. Scurvy is caused by a lack of vitamin C. Before the invention of refrigeration technology, it was hard to keep fruits and vegetables fresh on long voyages.

Your body needs vitamins. But what are they?

Some vitamins that the human body needs are produced within the body itself. But there are other vitamins we need to get from the foods we eat. This necessity is what makes a well-balanced diet so important.

Here are some important vitamins along with their source and their purpose in the body.

Vitamin	Source	Purpose
Vitamin A	Occurs naturally only in animal foods, such as eggs, liver, and milk	Important for bones, teeth, and skin
Vitamin D	Fatty fish; your skin also makes it when exposed to sunlight.	Prevents the bone disease rickets
Vitamin E	Seed oils, vegetable oils, wheat germs, and whole grains	Maintains *cell* membranes
Vitamin K	Cauliflower and green leafy vegetables; bacteria in your intestines can also make it.	Essential for blood clotting

BUILDING UP & BREAKING DOWN

DNA is the ultimate instruction manual for life. It is a complex *molecule* found in nearly every one of your living cells. DNA contains a unique code that dictates the formation, growth, and reproduction of cells and thus the body. It even directs the development of your bones, the body's framework.

In addition, DNA is the hereditary material by which offspring inherit traits from their parents. Through DNA, traits are passed down from one generation to the next. Do you look like your parents? It is because their DNA has been passed on to you!

You were once just one tiny *cell*. Through chemistry, that cell grew and multiplied—again and again—and now here you are!

RNA is DNA's partner—it is the messenger that carries DNA's instructions within the cell. RNA instructs tiny molecular factories called ribosomes to make different types of **proteins**. These proteins then carry out the work of the cell.

DNA is also involved in the breakdown of the body. Apoptosis is a process by which DNA directs the death of the cells.

Turns out that big molecule is a big deal!

DNA was discovered in 1868 by a Swiss biochemist, Friedrich Miescher. Scientists dismissed the molecule as unimportant until 1944, when a team headed by American geneticist **Oswald T. Avery** found evidence that DNA alone determined heredity.

Building up & breaking down

DNA's code

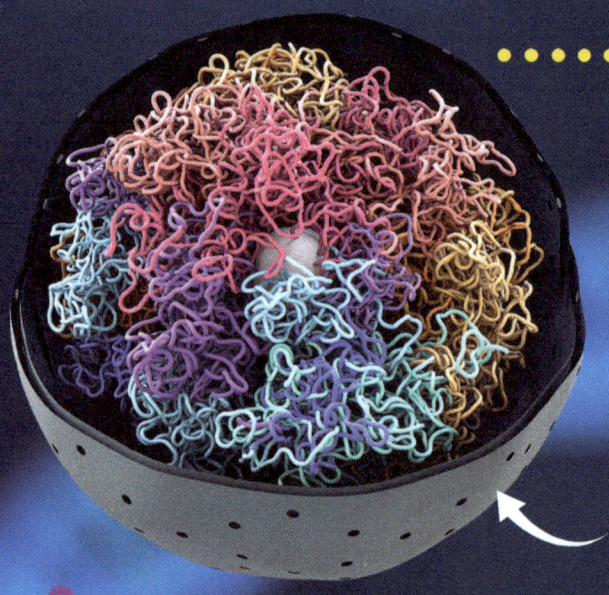
Cell nucleus

DNA is short for deoxyribonucleic *acid*. It is a thin, chainlike *molecule* made up of billions of *atoms*. DNA is found mainly in a highly coiled form within a cell's nucleus (center). Uncurled and stretched out, DNA is shaped like a twisted ladder—a double helix.

The ladder is made up of four building blocks called nucleotides. Each nucleotide consists of a sugar called deoxyribose joined to a phosphate and one of four compounds called bases. The bases are adenine (abbreviated A), cytosine (C), guanine (G), and thymine (T). Pairs of these bases form the "rungs" of the ladder. DNA's instructions are encoded in the sequence of these bases.

DNA is your body's instruction manual for building *cells,* tissues, and organs. Without DNA, you couldn't exist.

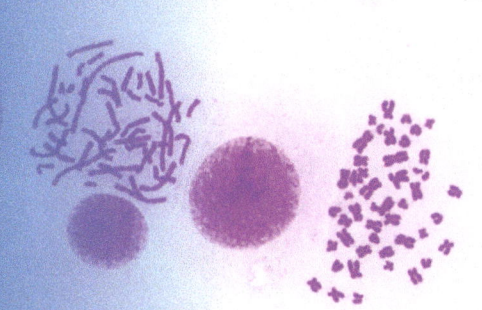

Your cells regularly multiply by splitting in half. Before a cell divides, it duplicates each strand of its DNA. When the cell divides, both the offspring cells thus receive a complete copy of the parent's DNA.

 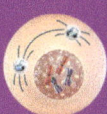 

Short sections of DNA called genes determine heredity—that is, the passing on of characteristics—in living things. The sequence of bases within a gene encodes instructions for assembling a protein from building blocks called amino acids.

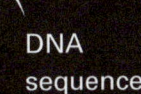
DNA sequence

CAREER CORNER

Studying human DNA advances our understanding in many areas of science. Testing someone's genes, for example, can reveal if they're at risk for certain diseases. You could advance our understanding of heredity by becoming a geneticist. Geneticists investigate the structure, function, and transmission of genes.

Building up & breaking down

RNA, the sidekick

Every superhero has a trusty sidekick. The sidekick might help fight villains, save lives, or even just drive the super-car. DNA's sidekick is ribonucleic acid—RNA. And like a good sidekick, RNA performs many functions. DNA can't run the cell alone. RNA *molecules* assist it in the production of *proteins*.

TECH TIME

In recent years, scientists have developed vaccines based on mRNA. For example, COVID-19 vaccines from the drug companies Moderna and Pfizer use special technology to carry lab-created mRNA into the body's cells. This mRNA contains instructions for making proteins that can help the cell to fight the virus. The future of mRNA vaccine tech is bright. Companies are working on mRNA vaccines for HIV, malaria, the flu—and even some cancers!

How exactly do your *cells* use *DNA?* RNA (ribonucleic *acid*) provides the other half of this puzzle.

As with DNA, molecules of RNA are chains of numerous smaller *chemical* units called nucleotides. The nucleotides are bound together chemically to form thin, chainlike molecules called polynucleotides. Each RNA molecule consists of only a single polynucleotide chain, however, unlike the double chain of DNA.

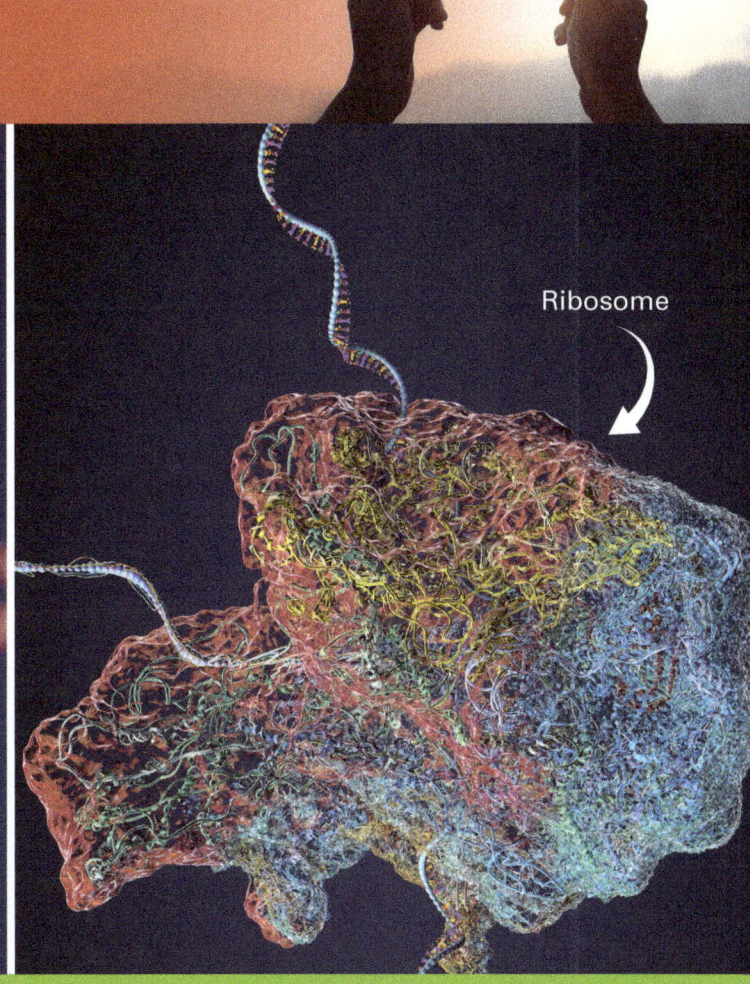

Ribosome

Different types of RNA perform different jobs. Some RNA molecules act as *enzymes* to speed up certain chemical *reactions*. Messenger RNA (mRNA) copies chemical instructions from DNA for making proteins. The mRNA then leaves the nucleus and carries the instructions to protein-making structures called ribosomes. These instructions tell the ribosome how to put amino acids together in the right order to make a specific protein. Transfer RNA (tRNA) collects amino acids and brings them to the ribosome for assembly. Ribosomes themselves contain another type of RNA called ribosomal RNA (rRNA).

Building up & breaking down

Building bones

Most of the body's tissues are soft, squishy, and flexible. Bone, strong and rigid, seems like the odd tissue out. But it's still a *tissue*, filled with proteins and cells!

About two-thirds of the weight of bone consists of minerals, mostly calcium, phosphate, and carbonate. The rest is organic material, largely a fibrous *protein* called collagen. A special type of *cell* called osteoblasts live in your bones, laying down collagen fibers and depositing minerals.

DID YOU KNOW?

Did you know that you have fewer bones than a newborn? It's true! Humans are born with 270 bones. But some of these bones fuse together as we age. By adulthood, we're usually down to 206 bones.

Bones provide your body's frame.
But where did your bones come from?

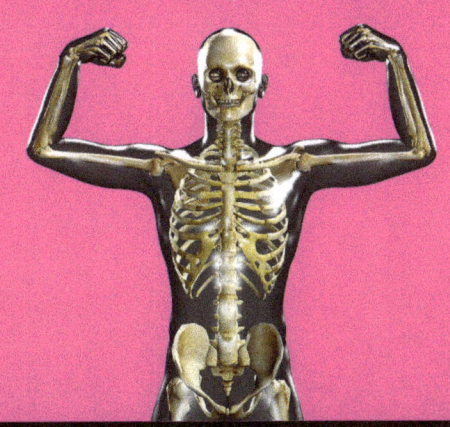

You had bones before you were born!
Bones begin to develop in the human embryo. These bones start out as soft connective tissue that hardens over time. Most bone tissue develops in a process called endochondral bone formation. In this process, a rubbery tissue called cartilage first replaces the soft connective tissue. Bone tissue in turn replaces the cartilage.

Throughout childhood, our bones continue to grow.
Long bones grow through a structure called the epiphyseal growth plate. The growth plate is a thin disk of cartilage near the end of a long bone. A new layer of bone successively replaces each layer of cartilage. In this way, the bone grows longer. The growth plate functions throughout childhood and adolescence and stops working when a person reaches adult height.

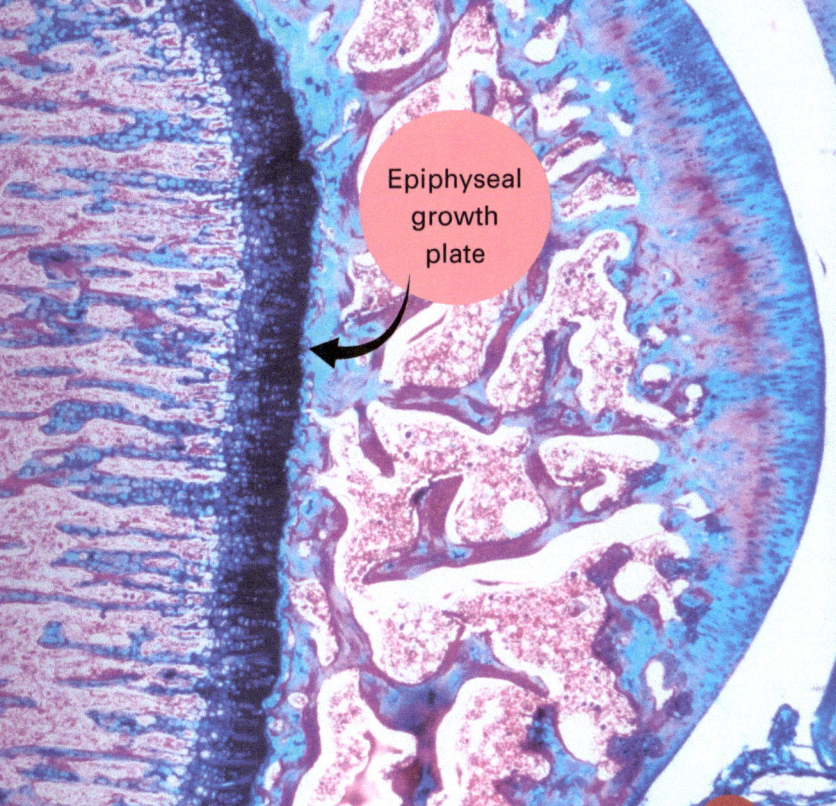

Epiphyseal growth plate

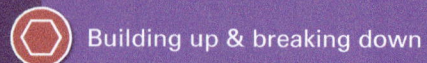
Building up & breaking down

Apoptosis

Apoptosis is a process that results in the controlled self-destruction of a cell. This genetically regulated process is an important part of normal growth and development.

Apoptic cell

Why would a living cell evolve to destroy itself? For the good of the organism! Apoptosis provides for the orderly elimination of unnecessary and worn-out cells. Older cells might no longer be functioning properly. In other cases, the function performed by a cell is no longer needed by the body. Apoptosis also plays a role in fighting certain diseases. For example, apoptosis can limit the uncontrolled division of cells that leads to cancer.

Cells contain genes that promote apoptosis, called proapoptotic genes. Genes that prevent apoptosis from occurring, called antiapoptotic genes, also exist in most cells. The balance between the activity of the two types of genes determines when and if a cell triggers its own death. Apoptosis can also be activated by external factors, such as X rays and certain drugs and hormones.

Cells don't last forever. In fact, they're programmed to self-destruct!

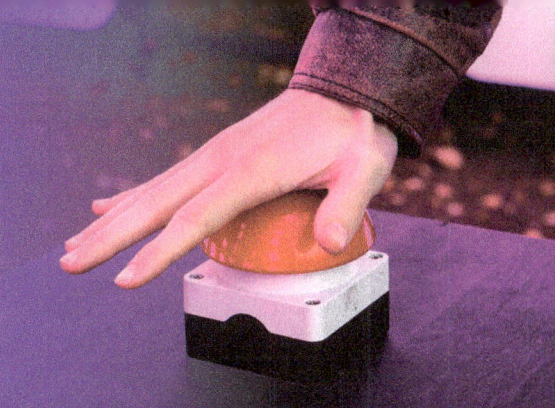

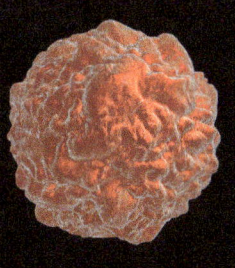 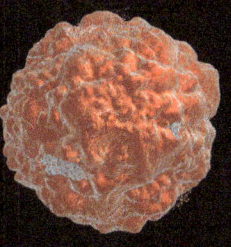 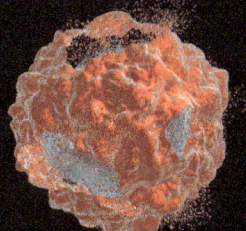
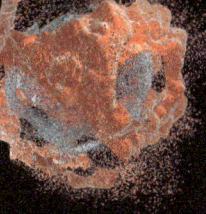 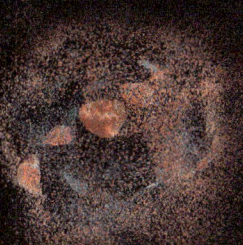

Several physical changes occur when a cell undergoes apoptosis. The cell shrinks, detaches from other cells, and breaks into particles called apoptotic bodies. Apoptotic bodies are then engulfed and digested by neighboring cells. This process prevents leakage of cell contents and inflammation, a reaction to cell damage.

Cell death isn't always a blessing. Many diseases and conditions can cause apoptosis, including viral infections, toxins (poisons), and oxygen deprivation.

TECH TIME

Manipulating apoptosis has incredible potential in the field of medicine. Scientists are working to develop drugs that prevent apoptosis when the process contributes to disease. They are also seeking to produce other drugs that promote apoptosis when the process is desired for killing cancer cells.

35

5
CHEMISTRY OF MEDICINE

One medicine commonly used across the world is aspirin. Aspirin, or acetylsalicylic *acid*, can help people with all sorts of ailments, including pain, fevers, and inflammation. Aspirin works by interacting with *enzymes* in the body. However, aspirin can cause stomach bleeding and other side effects.

Many medicines are made from or by living things. For example, antibiotics are used to fight infections caused by bacteria. These drugs attack bacterial cells while leaving the host animal's cells alone. An antibiotic called penicillin, for example, blocks the formation of *cell* walls in bacteria. This potent drug was discovered being produced by a lowly mold!

Penicillium mold

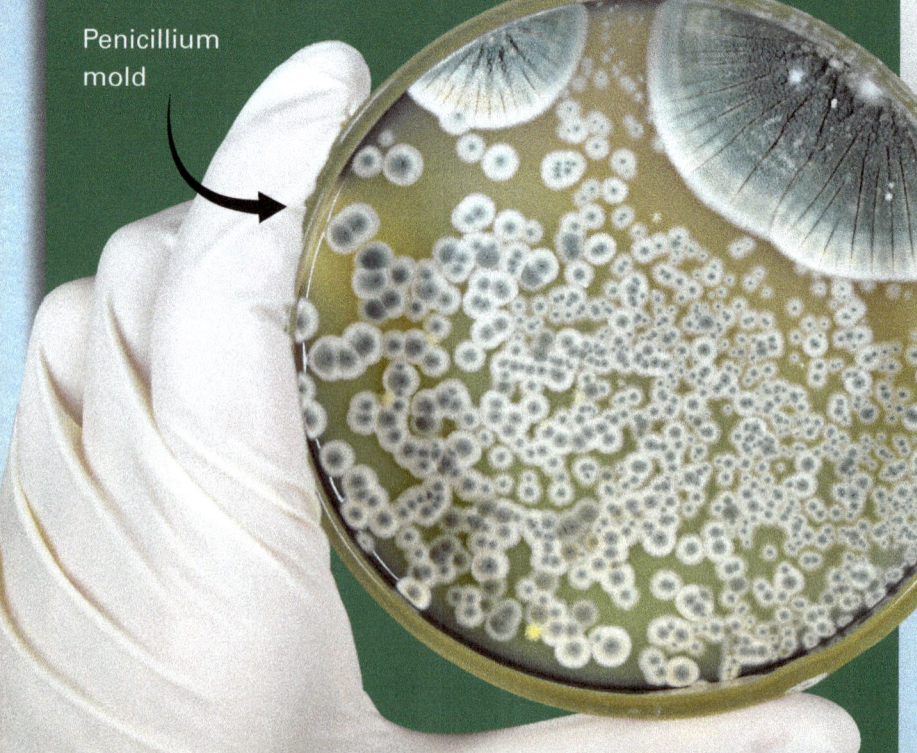

Modern medicine would be impossible without chemistry. Through the study of substances and *chemical reactions*, scientists have created treatments for terrible sicknesses.

36

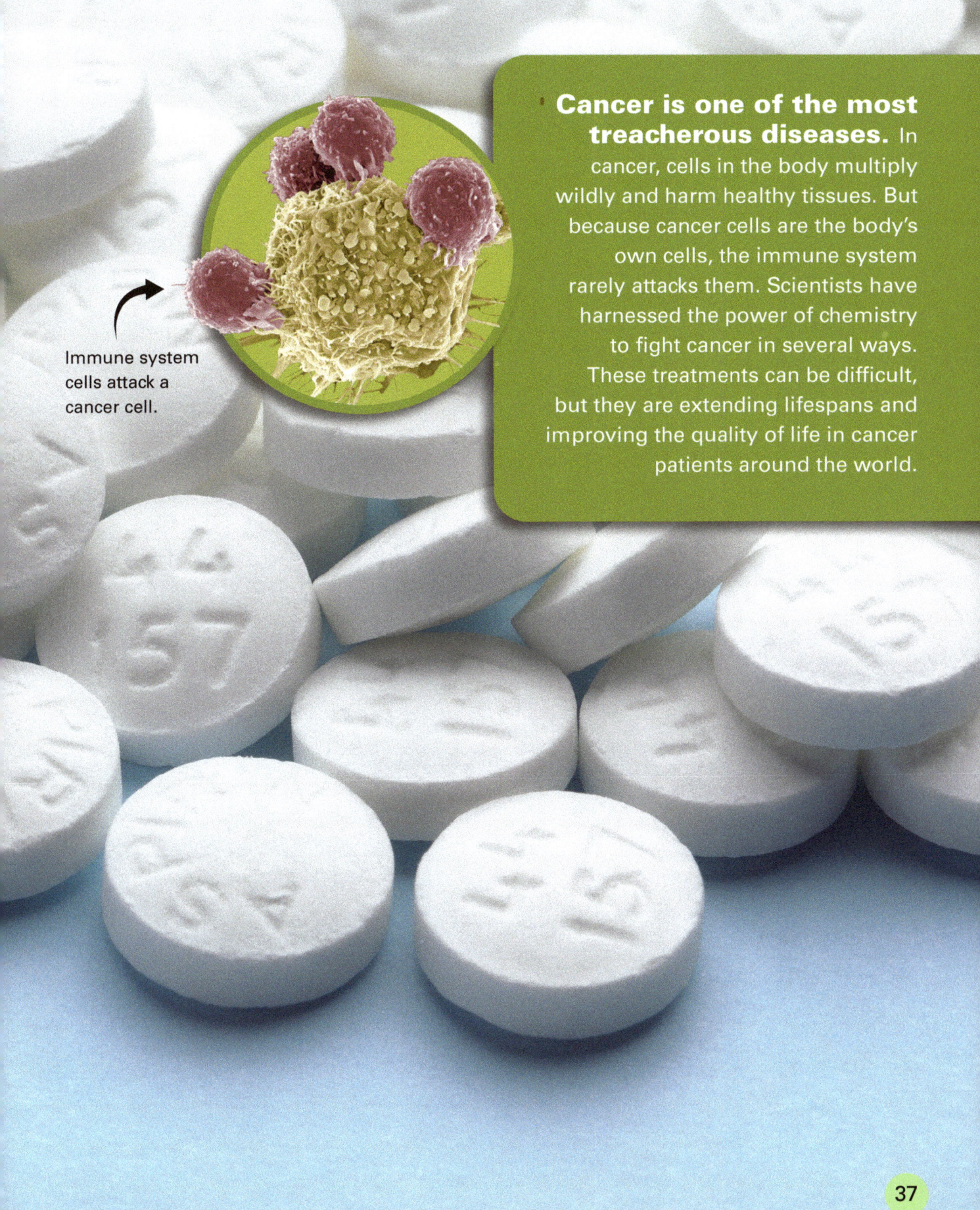

Immune system cells attack a cancer cell.

Cancer is one of the most treacherous diseases. In cancer, cells in the body multiply wildly and harm healthy tissues. But because cancer cells are the body's own cells, the immune system rarely attacks them. Scientists have harnessed the power of chemistry to fight cancer in several ways. These treatments can be difficult, but they are extending lifespans and improving the quality of life in cancer patients around the world.

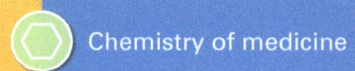
Chemistry of medicine

Aspirin

Aspirin (acetylsalicylic *acid*) helps relieve pain, lower fever from infections, and reduce inflammation due to illness or injury. Not only that, but aspirin also reduces blood clotting. So, it can be useful in preventing heart attacks, strokes, and other disorders that involve blood clots.

Aspirin is relatively safe when taken at the recommended dosage. However, it can irritate the stomach lining and cause stomach bleeding, a serious side effect particularly in the elderly. Children with chickenpox or influenza should not take aspirin.

Aspirin is one of the most used medicines in the world. Let's dive into the chemistry behind this wonder drug!

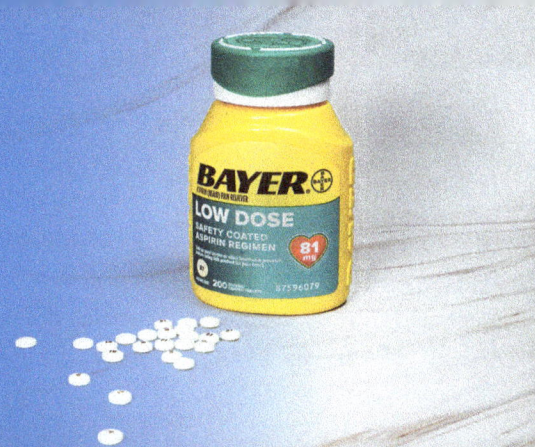

How does aspirin work? Aspirin is one of a class of drugs called nonsteroidal anti-inflammatory drugs (NSAID's). NSAID's work mainly by blocking the formation in the body of prostaglandins—biochemical compounds similar to hormones. Aspirin inactivates two *enzymes*, cyclooxygenase-1 and cyclooxygenase-2, which are necessary for the formation of prostaglandins.

Aspirin's *reactions* with the two enzymes have different effects in the body. When aspirin blocks cyclooxygenase-1, blood clotting and stomach lining irritation are reduced. In contrast, the inactivation of cyclooxygenase-2 reduces fever and inflammation.

Charles F. Gerhardt, a French chemist, first made acetylsalicylic acid in a laboratory in 1853. In 1897, the German chemist Felix Hoffmann found a new way to develop the compound while working for the *chemical* company Bayer.

Chemistry of medicine

Penicillin and antibiotics

The development of penicillin has had a tremendous impact on medicine. Different types of penicillin have played a major role in treating pneumonia, rheumatic fever, scarlet fever, and other diseases. The discovery also encouraged more research, leading to the discovery of many other antibiotics.

Penicillin comes from a type of mold named *Penicillium*. Chemists isolate some natural penicillin by processing Penicillium molds in various ways. They produce other forms, called semisynthetic penicillins, by changing natural penicillin substances through *chemical* processes. Penicillin G is the most widely used natural penicillin.

Penicillium mold under a light microscope

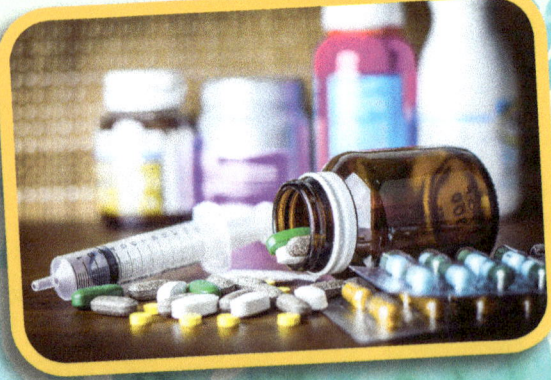

Penicillins kill bacteria by bonding with important *proteins* in the bacteria *cells*. This bonding prevents the formation of the stiff cell walls bacteria need to survive. Human cells do not form cell walls, so they remain undamaged by penicillins.

Most people who take penicillins experience no side effects, though some people suffer allergic *reactions*. These reactions are usually minor, causing fever or rashes. However, life-threatening reactions involving shock and breathing difficulties occur in some patients. Patients allergic to one form of penicillin will likely react to all forms.

Penicillin is a powerful drug used to treat infections caused by bacteria. It was the first successful antibiotic, a class of drugs produced by certain bacteria and fungi to disrupt rival cells.

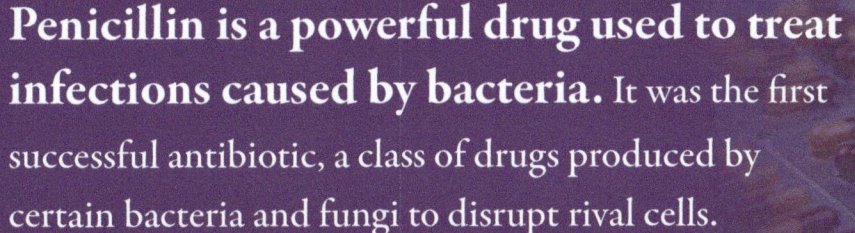

Mycobacterium tuberculosis bacteria, cause of the infectious disease tuberculosis

Since the discovery of penicillin, biochemists have developed a wide range of antibiotics. But, we must be careful with how we use them. Harmful bacteria can evolve resistance to different antibiotics, leading to waves of deadly infections.

Sir Alexander Fleming, a British scientist, discovered penicillin in 1928. But it remained a laboratory curiosity until 1939, when British researchers led by Howard Florey and Ernst Chain found a way to extract and purify penicillin from the mold. Mass production quickly followed—and just in time, too, as World War II (1939-1945) was sweeping the globe. Penicillin saved countless thousands of wounded soldiers from deadly infections during the war.

Chemotherapy

Doctors have a limited toolkit for dealing with cancers. Sometimes, surgeons can remove cancerous tissue. Other times, directed beams of radiation can shrink the cancer. But the best and most versatile method to reverse this deadly condition is chemotherapy. Chemotherapy is the treatment of cancers or infections with drugs that have a toxic effect on the cause of the illness.

Ideally, chemotherapy is selectively toxic—that is, the drugs poison cancer cells without harming healthy cells. It is most selectively toxic when it attacks diseases through a chemical process that does not occur in healthy cells. Think about penicillin. You just learned that it prevents bacteria from building their stiff cell walls. Animal cells do not form cell walls, so penicillin is selectively toxic to bacteria.

TECH TIME

Radiation therapy is another method to treat cancer. In radiation therapy, a machine attacks cancer cells with X rays or other high-energy particles from radioactive substances. While radiation kills cancer cells, it also kills normal cells. Specialists work to reduce side effects by shaping the radiation beam to affect the smallest possible area.

In cancer, the body's own cells turn against it. Chemotherapy—literally, chemical treatment—is one of the most effective methods that medicine has for treating cancer. It has serious side effects, however.

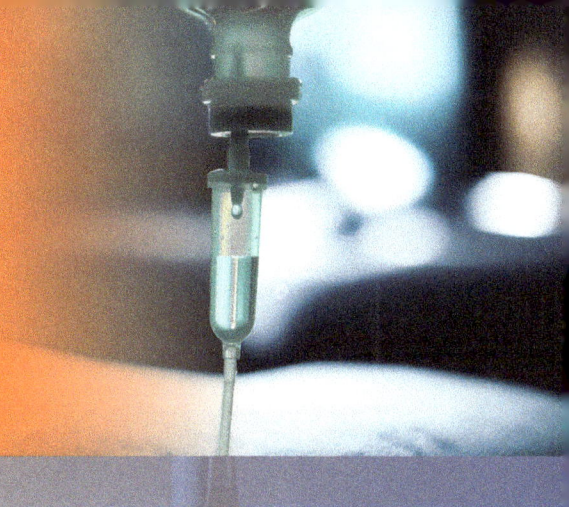

Unfortunately, because cancer cells are body cells, there are fewer differing features to selectively target. As a workaround, many chemotherapy drugs interfere with cell division. This strategy can be effective because cancer cells divide much more rapidly than normal cells. But many healthy cell types also divide rapidly, including those that line the digestive tract and those that form hair. The death of these and other normal cells during chemotherapy can result in nausea, hair loss, decreased resistance to disease, and other troublesome side effects.

Effective chemotherapy usually involves a combination of drugs. Doctors combine drugs that have different methods of acting on cancer cells and that produce different side effects. Combination therapy reduces the chance that cancer cells will develop resistance to the drugs. It also helps avoid serious side effects from large doses of a single drug.

An egg-shell-ent experiment

You will need:

- Several different types of beverages. Water, milk, soda, juice, or coffee are good options.
- A clear cup for each type of beverage
- One hard-boiled white egg, with shell, for each beverage you'd like to use
- A marker to write on the cups
- Toothbrush
- Toothpaste

Give it a try

1. Pour your beverages into your plastic cups
2. Label your plastic cups by their beverage
3. Place one hard-boiled egg, with shell, into each cup
4. Wait 48 hours
5. Compare the eggs
6. Brush the eggs with your toothbrush and toothpaste

You've learned about the chemical reactions that happen every day inside of your body. Let's do an experiment similar to one of those reactions!

Try this next!

These eggshells mimicked the chemical impact of beverages on your teeth. Once you finish with your beverages, why not try different beverages to see their impact? You could also use different methods of cleaning the eggs to see what works better or worse than a toothbrush with toothpaste.

QUESTION TIME!

Eggshells are chemically similar to the enamel that covers your teeth. What chemical reaction, which was discussed in this book, is most similar to the chemical reaction that happened to these eggs? Why do you think some beverages had a larger impact on the eggshells than other beverages? What does this tell you about protecting your teeth?

Index

A
adenosine triphosphate (ATP), 14-15
allergic reactions, 40
Al-Rāzī, 11
amino acids, 20, 22, 29, 31
antibiotics, 36, 40-41
apoptosis, 27, 34-35
artificial blood, 17
aspirin, 36, 38-39
Avery, Oswald T., 27

B
bacteria, 9, 25, 36, 40-42
bases, in DNA, 28-29
bile, 8, 19, 21
bones, 23, 25-26, 32-33

C
cancer, 30, 34-35, 37, 42-43
carbon dioxide, 15, 17
cartilage, 33
cell walls, 36, 40, 42
Chain, Ernst, 41

chemotherapy, 42-43
chlorine, 11
collagen, 32

D
deoxyribonucleic acid (DNA), 5, 26-31
digestion, 5-10, 19, 21, 35
division of cells, 29, 34, 43

E
electron transport chain, 15
enzymes, 8-9, 17, 21, 23, 31, 36, 39
esophagus, 6, 9-10
exercise, 14

F
fats, 8-9, 19, 21
Fleming, Sir Alexander, 41
Florey, Howard, 41

G
geneticist (career), 29
Gerhardt, Charles F., 39
glucose, 13-15, 20, 22
glycogen, 20
glycolysis, 14-15

H
hemoglobin, 12, 16-17
heredity, 26-27, 29

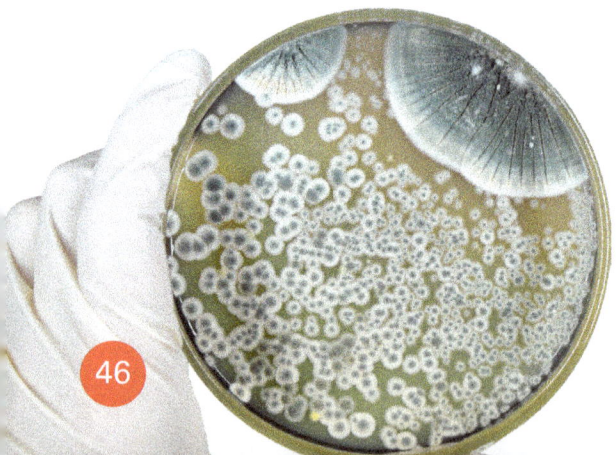

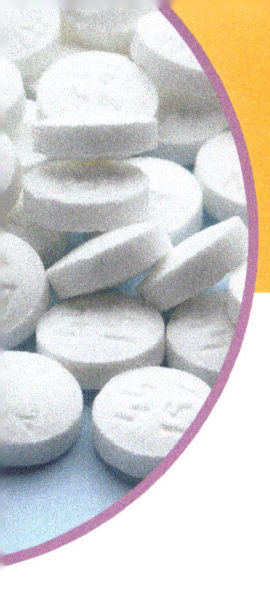

Hoffmann, Felix, 39
hydrochloric acid (HCl), 6, 9-11
hydrogen, 7, 11, 15

I
intestines, 6, 8-9, 21, 25
iron, 16, 21

K
kidney stones, 23
kidneys, 19, 22-23
Krebs cycle, 14-15

L
lactic acid, 14
liver, 8, 18-21, 25

M
malaria, 17, 30
messenger RNA (mRNA), 30-31
Miescher, Friedrich, 27
mitochondria, 15

N
nucleotides, 28, 31
nucleus of a cell, 28, 31
nutrition, 9

O
oxygen, 7, 12-18, 35

P
penicillin, 36, 40-42

R
radiation, 42
red blood cells, 12-13, 16-17, 23
respiration, cellular, 13-15
ribonucleic acid (RNA), 27, 30-31
ribosomes, 27, 31

S
scurvy, 24
sickle cell disease (SCD), 17
stomach, 6-11, 21, 36, 38-39

T
transfer RNA (tRNA), 31

U
urine, 19, 22-23

V
vaccines, 30
vitamins, 19, 21, 23-25

W
water, 7, 11, 13, 15, 18, 22

Glossary

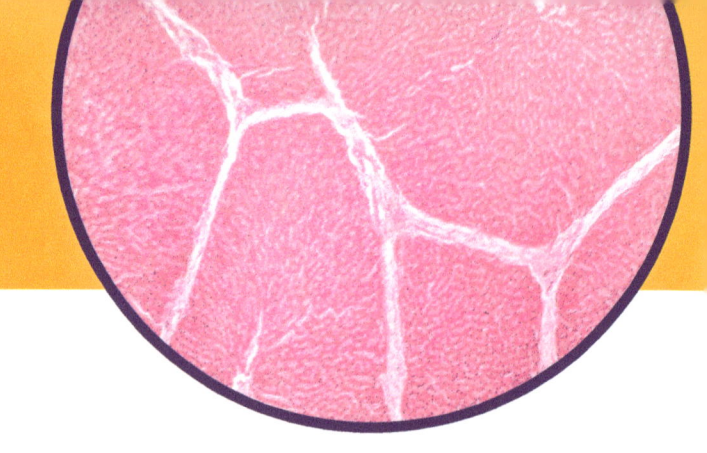

acid (AS ihd)—a type of molecule known by its special properties; it gives up a hydrogen atom in reactions

atom (AT uhm)—an incredibly tiny particle that makes up all things

cell (sehl)—the basic unit of all life; all organisms (living things) are made up of one or more cells

chemical (KEHM uh kuhl)—any of the many substances that make up the world's materials; of or having to do with chemistry

DNA—a thin, chainlike molecule found in every living cell on Earth that directs the formation, growth, and reproduction of cells and organisms

enzyme (EHN zym)—a molecule that speeds up chemical reactions in all living things

glucose (GLOO kohs)—a kind of sugar occurring in plant and animal tissues

hemoglobin (HEE muh GLOH buhn)—a substance in blood made up of iron and protein; it carries oxygen from the lungs to the tissues and some of the carbon dioxide from the tissues to the lungs

hydrogen (HY druh juhn)—the most abundant element; a colorless, odorless gas that burns easily

molecule (MOL uh kyool)—a group of joined atoms

organ (AWR guhn)—any part of an animal or plant that is composed of various tissues organized to do certain things in life

oxygen (OK suh juhn)—an element that nearly all living things need to survive; a gas without color, odor, or taste that forms about one-fifth of the air

protein (PROH teen)—chains of smaller organic molecules known as amino acids; the body uses proteins to build cells and to carry out the cells' work.

reaction (ree AK shuhn)—a process by which one or more molecules are converted into one or more different molecules

RNA—a complex molecule that helps produce substances called proteins

tissue (TIHSH oo)—a group of similar cells that work together with intercellular substances

water (WAWT uhr)—a transparent, colorless, tasteless, odorless compound of hydrogen and oxygen that is necessary for life

www.ingramcontent.com/pod-product-compliance
Lightning Source LLC
Chambersburg PA
CBHW061253170426
43191CB00041B/2418